Great birding, Always!

Jack Curran
Nov-2008

D1172068

Defensive parents protect young the morning after they hatched.

JACK CURRAN'S
WORLD OF BIRDS

PUBLISHED BY TAWNY OAKS PRESS

Copyright 2008 by Jack Curran
Permission to use any or all portions of this book
is granted provided the author is given credit
in the media in which it is used.

Edited by Elizabeth Ann Baker
Gregory L. Zarcoff, printing coordinator

Printed in China

Photo by Ann Viessman

Curran, Jack, 1935 -

**Jack Curran's WORLD OF BIRDS
A portfolio of photographs, watercolors and
wood carvings, with commentary on
forty years of bird observations
ISBN 1-4243-1084-9**

ACKNOWLEDGEMENTS

So many people have influenced me, taught me and encouraged me throughout my career that I feel the need to acknowledge them here, for without them there would be no book. In the second grade my teacher Mrs. Lampman, told me when I grew up I would be a commercial artist. She died before I could thank her for her insight. Miss Florence Power, my highschool art teacher, taught me the elements of design and the proper use of, and how to correctly mix, colors.

My classwork in fine art in Omaha at the University of Nebraska, under professors Peter Hill and Dr. John Blackwell, gave me a good understanding of art history and the many schools of art. One thing that particularly trained me in photography was the assignment to take pictures for the art department of historical works of art for the school's archives. I purchased my first 35mm single lens reflex camera at a pawn shop in 1957.

During my 20 years at the Nebraska Game and Parks Commission, Gene Mahoney and Rex Amack, both of whom were directors of the agency, allowed me, while I was art director for NEBRASKAland magazine, the freedom to branch out into radio, television, film, multi- media and special projects.

For the past 25 years the patrons who purchased my prints, bird carvings, brick art and, finally, the monumental bronze buffalo for the Omaha zoo are the one's who encouraged me by supporting me personally and financially.

Mike Yanney raised the money for my first brick sculpture commission. Harold Andersen showcased my work in the Omaha World Herald. Stan and Roger Judd allowed me to sculpt at Endicott clay products in Fairbury for twenty years. Amy Scott and Dr. Lee Simmons trusted me to create the bronze buffalo.

While I had many, many patrons, Dr. and Mrs. David Kettleson, Mr. and Mrs. Harry Alward and Mr. and Mrs. Gary Gish need special mention. To them and everyone else who supported me, I say "Thanks."

One- day- old canada goslings. I watched the nest daily for two weeks.

INTRODUCTION

While I have no formal schooling in ornithology, I have made it a life-long endeavor to become a true bird watcher, not just a birder and not a lister (someone who keeps a list of every bird species they see, if only for a fleeting moment).

This book is not a technical or scientific work. It is a collection of my bird art, photographs and observations that I leave as inspiration and encouragement to others who might develop an interest in birds.

While working at the Nebraska Game and Parks Commission, I spent much of my own time photographing birds. My basement also served as a studio where I brought game farm duck subjects. The wildlife biologists generously shared what they knew about both game birds and non-game birds. I became the third falconer licensed in Nebraska and worked with a raptor recovery center.

Every photo I took belonged to NEBRASKAland Magazine, so I had virtually no images that I could call my own. After moving to Arkansas in 1995, the woodlands around my home inspired me to again take up photography. By that time, digital camera technology had improved enough to challenge film images.

Probably the best motivator has been a pair of Red-shouldered Hawks that nest in my yard and hunt frogs in my ponds. I bought the latest Nikon equipment and started photographing in earnest. All of my photos have been taken in Arkansas, Florida, Kansas, Iowa and Nebraska.

I dedicate this book to my wife, Marilyn, who, after 50 years still tolerates my love for birds, even though she often calls me "one dimensional." Although our time together here is growing short, we thank the Lord for the years he has given us.

CONTENTS

Least Bittern

Great Blue Heron

NORTH AMERICAN WATERFOWL

How do we learn to tell one duck from another? Typically, upon seeing a new duck, the viewer goes to a field guide and searches until a name can be attached to the duck. In my case, still a teenager, the first duck I could identify other than a Mallard was the little Blue-winged Teal. I saw my first one while walking on the banks of the Papio creek near Omaha, with my cousin Bill. This colorful duck has influenced my art ever since.

My first four woodcarvings were of the Blue-winged Teal (see page 137). Of course, I knew the Mallard—almost everyone can identify it with its green head and white neck ring. Once, my uncle Jim shot a bird with a green head. We thought it was a mallard. Turned out that it was a Common Merganser. What a let down.

If you look at the range map for the blue-wings, you'll see they have the largest nesting range of any north american duck other than the adaptable mallard. And while blue-wings are fairly common throughout most of the country, surprisingly, not many people are familiar with this little acrobatic flier.

I can vividly remember the first time I saw a small flock of Northern Shovelers lift off of a shallow pond in 1972. I thought they were Mallards. After some research, I had learned the name of another duck species. I think the beautiful Wood Duck was the next to get a name.

Working for NEBRASKAland magazine as Art Director helped stimulate my desire to learn waterfowl. While a duck might be easy to identify in the spring during breeding, fall is a different thing. After a spring molt, male ducks look more like hens. Fall ducks are in a transitional phase, when new breeding or nuptual feathers are replacing those of summer.

There are several classifications of ducks. "Dabblers" and "divers" are the most common. Dabblers are most often seen feeding in shallow water near the shore, sometimes by tipping with their tail above the water and only their heads under water. Included in this group are; Mallards, Pintails, Gadwall and Wigeon. Some dabblers like the Teal and Shovelers, strain mud through rakes in their bills. After a little time in the field, dabblers are easy.

Divers, on the other hand, feed in deeper water, going completely under, only to resurface later some distance away. The most well-known of the divers are Canvasback, Redhead, Goldeneye, Scaup, Ring-necked and Bufflehead. The other types of ducks include perching, whistling, eiders, sea ducks, mergansers and stifftails. There is much to learn about ducks.

In addition to ducks, geese and swans make up a large part of the waterfowl world. Canada Geese are the most widespread and most familiar in the United States. Other less-known species are Barnacle, Brant, White-fronted, Ross's and the Snow Goose populations. Blue Geese are a morph or color variation of the Snow Goose. We have three swan species; the Trumpeter, Tundra and Mute. Some of these birds have six foot wing spans.

The Giant Canada Geese have been re-introduced to the wetlands that they originally inhabited during the pioneer days. Hungry settlers, who found them an easy target because they flew low and slow, almost anihilated them completely. Through management, their numbers have increased dramatically. It is not unusual for geese to live for more than 20 years. An old-time game biologist told me that geese are one of the only game birds that can be stockpiled. Pheasants, quail and doves have an average life span between one and four years.

Canada geese can be difficult to identify since there are at least six sub-species in the same family. The largest is the *maxima* or giant, and the smallest are the Cackling and Richardson's. These small geese have very short bills. With so much mixed breeding, it is very difficult to tell them apart, either flying or on the water.

In the early days of the pioneers, there were vast numbers of waterfowl. Settlers and market hunters reduced waterfowl and shorebird numbers to critical levels. Thankfully, modern game management practices combined with the efforts of hunting and conservation groups, have provided much-needed critical nesting habitat, thereby stabilizing waterfowl numbers. The population of Snow Geese have exploded to where hunters have been asked to help lower their numbers.

My only limited edition print. The original is owned by my nephew, Tom Curran, Yankton, South Dakota.

I used this pen and ink drawing on my letterheads for many years. My first four wood carvings were of the demure little blue-wing. It truly is my favorite duck.

At first glance, one would know that this is a Canada goose. In a mixed flock, it would be easy to see that this goose is a little smaller than the lesser canada goose...and it has the small bill, indicating that it is probably a Richardson's Goose. Even smaller is the Cackling Goose, whose breast is darker with a purplish sheen. While the richardson's is seen in the central flyway states, the "cackler" resides primarily on the west coast.

It is easy to see why the Wood Duck, pictured above, is considered our most colorful duck. This species, too, was on the threatened list in the 1900's. The passage of the Migratory Bird Treaty Act of 1918 is credited with saving this bird from extinction. Once it was found only east of the Missouri River, but today it inhabits all but the most moutainous areas of the country. Its recovery is a tribute to man's concern about waterfowl. Each year, conservation groups and boy scouts make and place thousands of nesting boxes, needed to replace all of the natural nesting cavities that have been destroyed over the years.

This pair of resting geese on the left are examples of the Giant Canadas. Their bills are much longer and they can weigh 20 pounds or more. The Richardson's will weigh around 5 pounds and the Lessers somewhere in between. There are many different breeding populations of Canada Geese all across North America.

Ross's Geese are much smaller than Snow Geese. While they look alike, the main difference is size and a smaller bill. Some sources estimate their population, which was about 6,000 birds in 1935, now to be 800,000 birds. Most winter in the Sacramento valley of California but they are moving east rapidly. Some Ross's interbreed with lesser Snow Geese.

At one time, a darker colored goose was called a Blue goose. Now, biologists recognize this to be a color "morph" of the Snow Goose. The dark color is considered to be dominant, so if a blue goose mates with a white goose, some of the off-spring will be dark. If two white birds mate, the offspring will be white. Two darks mating will have mostly dark young.

The sound of Snow Geese lifting off can be both exhilarating and deafening. Two things contribute to the tremendous population explosion. Federal and State waterfowl refuges protect the birds from hunters. Both harvested and newly planted fields provide ample food for wintering flocks which assures that they will arrive at their overcrowded and over-grazed breeding grounds in good condition. These birds were feeding on tender rice plants in southeastern Arkansas.

Canada Geese are also increasing in numbers, but for different reasons. This game bird has easily adapted to urban life. They thrive on city lakes and golf course ponds, fully protected from hunting. In some communities they have become a nuisance to the point where local residents call wildlife managers to disperse the birds. For most people, hunting or killing the geese is not an option. As the problem increases, some drastic measures will have to be implemented by game biologists.

This is a photo of a Green- winged Teal drake taken in my basement. I built a fiberglas tub, enclosing it with masonite and a habitat background. These photos were used for woodcarving reference. His plumage was just coming out of the transitional stage. I kept this bird for two months. Also had a pair of Cinnamon Teal on loan from Bill Lemburg of Cairo, Nebraska. Bill had the knack of being able to breed birds that normally would not breed in captivity.

Scaup are sometimes called "butterballs" by the old-time hunters. Watching them fly is a real treat. This is the Lesser Scaup. The Greater Scaup is slightly larger and often prefers salt water. Up close, you'll see more purple on the head of the Lesser and more green on the head of the Greater. They spend much time in large groups on open bodies of water. Males often outnumber females three to one. They are almost as abundant as Mallards.

In the fall and winter, both male and female Ruddy Ducks are similar, but the male has more color in the spring. Ruddies are seldom seen flying...preferring to dive when escaping from danger.

From the first time I saw a photo of a Ruddy Duck, and heard about its courtship antics, it became a goal of mine to see it for myself. Ruddies are one of the many species nesting at Crescent Lake Wildlife Refuge in the Sandhills of Nebraska. I made the trip in 1980.

A marsh can be a scary place for a first timer by himself. Its dark when you get there, and you need to carry a bucket to sit on and camo netting to hide in.... plus your camera and tripod...and maybe something to drink and snack on—You might be there for three or four hours—and all you can do is hope that the ruddies will swim back into the little bay where they were the morning before. It's difficult plodding through the reeds and a lake bottom of stinky sludge and mud.

Even before the sun came over the horizon, the marsh was alive with the sounds of it's residents...everything from rails to bitterns, sometimes called thunder pumpers" and Yellow- headed Blackbirds. I happened to pick a spot too close to a Coot —she squawked all the time I was there. Only after a baby Coot swam into my hand under the netting did I realize that the Coot nest was just five feet away. I wondered if it wasn't dangerous for the baby to sport all that color.

Out of the corner of my eye, I saw a male Ruddy swim into the bay. He put on quite a show, pumping his bill against his breast with a low call timed to his thumping sound.

Ruddies nest in thick vegetation of reeds or cattails where the water is about 10 inches deep. Their nest begins at the bottom and is built above the water line—and it keeps getting larger as eggs are laid. These stubby little ducks have the reputation of laying eggs in other nests. A wandering female can lay up to 60 eggs in a season.

The Ruddy Duck belongs to an unusual group of waterfowl known as *stifftails*. Of six different species, three are in the Americas, one in Eurasia, one in Africa and one in Australia. There are three races of the Ruddy Duck—one in the US, and two in South America. We also have the Masked duck, which is very elusive and seldom seen. It has moved north from South America, Panama and Costa Rica.

The male Ruddy Duck sports this breeding plumage from early spring to August. During his nuptial display, he throws his head back, swims vigorousy with stiff tail upright and proceeds to thump his bill on his chest. I have been less than 10 feet from a displaying male. It is like nothing else you will ever witness. Only the dance of the Western Grebe is more spectacular. 50 percent of Ruddy Ducks winter on the West Coast. The rest winter in southern states and the East Coast. They mostly migrate at night, so are rarely seen flying.

The Bufflehead duck is the smallest of the divers. They usually travel in pairs, or flocks of five to ten birds. The white on the head is similar to that of the Hooded Merganser. The female is all black and brown with a small white patch behind the eye. These monogamous little ducks are small enough to nest in old flicker and woodpecker holes. Buffleheads are the fastest fliers of all ducks and migrate in every flyway in the United States.

Some experts say that the Ring-necked Duck is misnamed as the rusty-colored ring around the neck is difficult to see. A more appropriate name would be Ring-billed. These fast fliers are more usually seen in groups of twenty or less. They nest in the northern states and Canada, preferring small tree-lined lakes and open marshes. The nests are often placed in grassy areas near water and the female continues to build it while laying up to a dozen eggs.

This Mallard hen was resting at the edge of a lake, and although wild, she was pretty tolerant of my encroachment into her space and allowed me to get close enough for this photo. Mallards are the most numerous of all duck species in the United States. On some residential lakes they almost become domesticated, often breeding with the domestic Muscovy Duck. The current wild Mallard breeding population is estimated at 10 million birds. It has varied from 12 million to 6 million.

Mallard drakes enter their first molt in June, resembling hens until September when they begin to acquire the nuptial or breeding plumage we are all familiar with—a green head with a white ring around the neck. This photo was taken in October. Some late- hatched drakes still show their hen- like plumage until mid- November. In the spring, it is not unusual to see three or more drakes vying for one hen. Even though hunters avoid shooting hens, drakes still outnumber them.

In the 1960's the Trumpeter Swan was considered for the federal list of endangered species. After a flock of 2,000 trumpeters was discovered in Alaska it was taken off of the list. Various states lisited them as state- endangered or state- threatened. Several states have been sucessful with restoration programs. Nebraska now again has trumpeters nesting on many scenic sandhill lakes. Arkansas is working with Iowa to establish another wintering flock like the one near Heber Springs.

When I first saw this pair swimming on a pond in Florida, I thought they were Black Ducks, but later I realized they fit the description of Mottled Ducks. Both species are related to the Mallard but both males and females have the same plumage. The bill on the female is almost identical to the female Mallard's bill. Black Ducks are darker overall. The Mottled Duck pretty much hugs the East Coast while the Black Duck can be found throughout the eastern half of the United States.

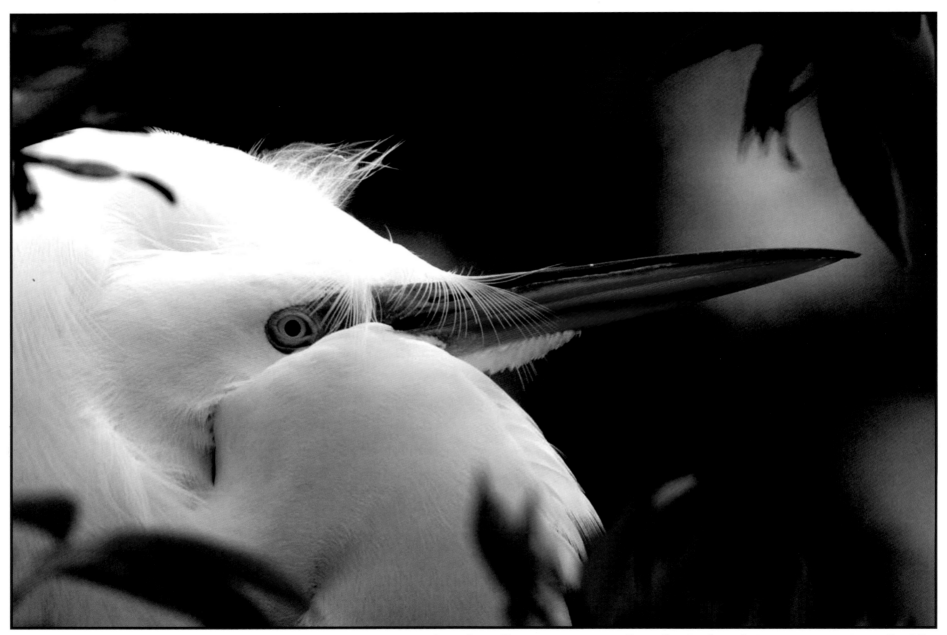

It is very unsual to get this close to a nesting Great Egret, but the Alligator Farm and Zoological Park in St. Augustine, Florida, provides nesting sites for most of the egrets and herons. An elevated walkway allows visitors the chance to get closer to incubating birds. Alligators prevent nest robbers from climbing the trees. The green colored "lores" appear during the breeding season, otherwise they are more yellow. Both of these images were selected as a Birder's World Photo of the Week."

WADING BIRDS

Typically, wading birds have long legs and long necks. The waders include some strange bedfellows like storks, limpkins, rails, egrets, herons, bitterns, ibis, spoonbills, cranes, flamingos and gallinules. Almost all of these species can be seen in Florida and Texas, but more than a few migrate northward during the nesting season.

I saw my first Cattle Egret in Jamaica many years ago. In less than ten years, they had expanded their range to Nebraska. Originally residents of Africa, Cattle Egrets flew across the Atlantic Ocean, possibly during a storm, to settle in northern South America. Then colonies slowly moved northward to the United States. Often seen around cattle, they feed on insects.

So, too, have other birds, like the ibis and spoonbill, been reported in several northern states. Herons seem to be growing in number. I see many new rookeries along our local streams. After twelve years, Great Blue Herons have discovered the little ponds in my tree-covered yard to feast on my Koi fish.
I have spent countless hours observing the waders—probably the most difficult to see are the little rails. Unfortunately, the first rail I ever saw was hanging dead from a barbed wire fence. At first, the identity of this little bird was a mystery to me, but a little research showed it to be a Sora rail.

Of all the waders, the Sandhill Cranes make the biggest impression on me. They migrate by the thousands from Texas and New Mexico to Nebraska's Platte River valley. There they will spend a month or more gaining much needed weight before continuing northward to their nesting grounds in April.

Just recently, I saw my first White-faced Ibis at a fish hatchery pond, 15 miles from my home in Arkansas. As usual when sighting an unfamiliar bird, I had to research my field guide to find the correct name. It's always a good idea to carry some good binoculars that will help you to get a closer look at the specific characteristics needed to identify your subject.

While all the waders have different shapes and sizes, they co-exist in those swamps, marshes and streams that provide an ample supply of fish, amphibians, crustacea and insects. Overpopulation in traditional habitats would probably explain why birds have expanded to other states. Non-game biologists are continually monitoring the population dynamics of waders, looking for possible problems and positive solutions.

Most egrets develop spectacular plumes to help the birds display during courtship. At one time, demand for plumes to adorn women's attire severely affected populations. Laws and public awareness saved them.

This juvenile Snowy Egret spent the month of September just a few blocks from my house on Sugar Creek. Great Egrets, Green Herons and Great Blue Herons also frequent the creek in late autumn. The legs of this bird are pale green with some black showing. I spent one whole day trying to hide in the trees, then stalk this little creature. While I saw this bird many times during the month, I only attempted to get close one enjoyable day. With quiet patience and persistence, I succeeded.

A Snowy Egret fishes intently during the peak of breeding season in Florida. This bird was very tolerant of me as I took several photos in the late afternoon. While the feet are yellow, the rest of the legs are black. The bill, too, is black and the lores are dark yellow- orange. This bird is smaller than the Great Egret, with a wing span of about 41 inches compared to 51 inches. They are more widely distributed in the United States than the Great Egret but not of the Great Blue Heron.

Thought it would be challenging and fun to try some flight shots of Great Blue Herons on Lake Bella Vista, where they spend a lot of time fishing in the shallows. In a couple of hours, I was fortunate to get some decent shots. It was difficult to pick the ones to include in the book. Once, in 1979, I set up a 50 foot scaffold on a heronry located in the Nebraska Sandhills. When the trees leafed out, I couldn't see the nests. All that effort and no photos or film to show for it.

On a dark, rainy, overcast day, this Great Blue Heron flew under the clouds, only to discover my Koi ponds exposed by relatively leafless woodlands. I happend to look out my office window, just 20 feet from the colorful marauder. Grabbed my camera with the 80/400 millimeter zoom, carefully opened the window and had a great time taking pictures until it was time to scare it away. During nesting season, I keep an eye out for these crafty fishermen—they did kill two colorful Koi.

The Little Blue Heron has expanded its range over the years. It can be found on both coasts and as far north as Newfound-land. Even though it sports plumes during the breeding season, most agree that it escaped the ravages of the plume hunters. This little heron often nests in colonies with other egrets and herons. It prefers marshes, fresh-water lagoons and flooded pastures, but is equally at home in coastal areas as well.

For part of the first year, the Little Blue Heron sports all white plumage. As it molts into the blue-gray adult plumage, it goes through a mottled color phase. Even though the legs are greener, this bird can be confused with a juvenile Snowy Egret.

Observers of nesting colonies have noted that it is not unusual to see a female mate with several males in one day. The small and flimsy nests they build are easily destroyed by high winds.

The White Ibis travels and nests in great numbers. My first sighting of them was on a golf course in Jacksonville, Flori-
da. I tried many times to get close enough for a photo. This one finally cooperated in St. Augustine. He wasn't exactly
dressed to have his picture taken. It is a beautiful sight to behold when a flock flies against a deep blue sky. Like other
waders, they vary their diets, consuming almost anything they glean from the bottom of a lake or salty shoreline.

These birds sent me scurrying to my field guide. My first impression was that they were Glossy Ibis. By checking the range map, I saw that the White-faced Ibis would be more likely seen in Arkansas, just a few miles from my house on a state fish hatchery pond. While the white is not showing on the face, the red eyes are a giveaway to correct identification. These are the first ones I have ever seen. It is always exciting to add another bird to those you can identify.

The Wood Stork was once called the Wood Ibis. They forage in groups, opening their sensitive bills and waiting for a fish to pass through so they can catch them. This is the only North American stork.

This little bird has been renamed three times since I first saw one along the Missouri river in Nebraska. Once, it was called the Little Green Heron, then the Green- backed Heron and now, the American Birding Association has settled on Green Heron.

Once, on a nature trail, several people passed me without seeing the Green Heron on the left, even though it was only fifteen feet away. People are in such a big hurry, they rush to see what is beyond the next bend rather than enjoy the birds that are right next to them. What a pity. Thank goodness I saw it and got this photo. It's the closest I've ever been to one. Watching their stealthy hunting technique is a good study of patience and perseverance.

Some wildlife photographers specialize in flight shots. The critical thing to remember is to pan or move the camera with the bird while pressing down on the shutter release. A relatively fast shutter speed helps stop the motion of the wings. This heron was particularly cooperative, flying back and forth along a shoreline, which gave me many chances at it. Adult plumage makes an elegant statement. You can tell by the shadows that this was taken about three in the afternoon.

Most golfers seemed oblivious to the nesting activity of the Great Blue Herons just behind the green. This heronry in a big old sycamore was just three years old. It had over fifteen nests.

Sad to say, these nests are all gone now. The herons could not tolerate the myriad Turkey Vultures that began to roost in this same tree. One other heronry near a stream met the same fate. There is a photo of a roosting vulture on page 85.

An adult Black- crowned Night- Heron is a striking bird with its black, gray and white plumage. Almost a year old, this bird will one day be as regal as its parents when it loses these drab feathers and sports red eyes. These birds of the marsh are considered nocturnal, roosting during the day and foraging during dusk and dawn. These birds feed primarily on fish. This photo was taken in February at St. Marks National Wildlife refuge in Florida.

There are few areas in the world where the Cattle Egret has yet to take up residence. This adaptable bird can fish or forage for insects scared up by the hooves of cattle. They too, nest in large colonies—a Kenyan observer noted 1,000 nests in one colony.

This Yellow-crowned Night-Heron feeds primarily on crabs and crustaceans. In Oklahoma, the birds were seen to be gorging on grasshoppers. While mostly a coastal bird, they have been expanding inland.

Happy are the times when you come across a scene like this and have your camera at the ready. I was just out driving south of Jacksonville, looking for Least Terns when this pair of Snowy Egrets came into view. A window mount helped steady the camera, as the birds were probably eighty yards away. My 400 milimeter lens is equivalent to 600 milimeters on a 35mm film camera. Another digital bonus is that you can check your exposure and composition immediately.

One of my favorite birding haunts in Jacksonville is the Julington Creek development. There are little bodies of water all through the area. You can tell that this Great Egret is more interested in finding a meal than in how close I am. Other times, the bird flies off when I try to get too close. In this same spot, I got a great sequence of a Little Blue Heron catching and eating a sunfish. Wouldn't you know that an inexperienced technician failed to save the images on a CD for me. Drats!

Federal, state and local agencies are doing their best to increase Whooping Crane numbers. An unexpected storm killed 17 of the 18 cranes that made the trip to Florida in the fall of 2006. This whooper, still in immature plumage was not fit enough to be released into the wild. It now resides in the Jacksonville, Florida zoo where it has been paired with another crane. At maturity, 4 to 7 years away, it is hoped that the two will mate and successfully raise young.

This Sandhill Crane is also on display at the "JAX" zoo. Sandhill cranes are playing an important role in the effort to increase whooper populations. They incubate whooper eggs. Some have adopted whooper young who migrate with the Sandhill families. Because the courtship displays are so different, biologists are confident that the two species will not cross- breed. There are several different migrating and non- migrating populations of Sandhill Cranes in North America.

Florida has a large population of resident Sandhill Cranes. One major concentration is at Payne's Prairie, south of Gainesville. The birds have now taken to residential areas around golf courses. Home owners feed the birds so they become quite tolerant of human activity. The two photos shown here were taken at the country club golf course in June. These are probably non- breeders, which means that they are too young to breed. It takes two to six years to reach breeding maturity.

Mississippi also has a small non- migrating population of Sandhill Cranes. There are only approximately 100 birds left and the group's status is tenuous at best, even though there is much public concern. The resident population of Florida whoopers is estimated at about 80. Most of the mortality comes from predators, power lines and other unknown causes. In recent years, even during a severe drought, a few whoopers have been able to nest successfully and raise their chicks.

While sitting in a blind at the Rowe Sanctuary on the Platte River in Nebraska, I witnessed this unusual scene. With much tumult, the cranes landed in the shallows, preparing to roost for the night. After midnight the birds quit chattering and stood almost motionless in the water. The stark silence prompted me to open a window and take this six- second exposure.

My reservation for the blind was for April 2nd. Crane numbers peak the second and third weeks of March. By April 15th, virtually all the cranes have left for the northern nesting areas. The temperature this night dropped to 22 degrees, which meant that the cranes came to the river after sunset and left the river before sunrise, limiting photo opportunities.

No one really knows how long Sandhill Cranes have been visiting the Platte river each spring. Experts agree that the annual staging of the cranes probably has taken place for thousands of years. While the cranes winter in Texas, New Mexico and Colorado, 80 percent, or almost 500,000 of them, seem to funnel through central Nebraska on their way back north. It is assumed that the cranes use the stopover to gain needed weight, feeding on waste grain and crustaceans.

There is another population of Greater Sandhill Cranes that winter in California, returning north to Oregon and Idaho to nest and raise their young. Sandhill Crane populations have grown in recent years, even though a few states allow limited hunting. It is not unusual to see a Whooping Crane or two traveling with the "sandhillers." Wildlife managers hope to have several distinct populations of Whoopers so that one catastrophe will not decimate the entire species.

It is not unusual to see 20,000 cranes per mile of river during mid-March when crane numbers peak. Birdwatchers from all over the world visit central Nebraska to witness this migration spectacle. In addition to the cranes, thousands of geese and ducks use the wetlands in the nearby rainwater basin. It is truly an experience that first-time visitors will never forget. Many residents from Omaha and Lincoln make an annual trip to see the cranes.

Unless the two are standing together, it is difficult to distinguish the Lesser"from the Greater Sandhill Cranes. This may be a mixed flock since both groups are found on the Platte River staging area. Lessers are about five inches shorter, or 41 inches, while the Greaters are about 46 inches tall. The Lesser Sandhill Cranes nest farther north, up to Alaska where as the larger cousins nest in southern Canada and the northern United States. Some interbreeding probably occurs.

Audubon's Rowe Sanctuary is located on the Platte River south of Gibbon, Nebraska. They have improved the river channels to encourage more cranes to roost on this stretch of river. While they have public viewing blinds, I chose to rent a plywood box blind, 4 feet high, 4 feet wide and 8 feet long. The rangers locked me in at 3:30 in the afternoon and let me out at 11:30 AM the next day. There is no guarantee that any birds will land on sandbars in front of you. You hope they will.

Because it got colder the night I was in the blind, the cranes did not return to their river roost until after the sun had set. If the wind had been out of the east, the birds would have been flying toward me. In fact, the wind was very strong until about three hours later. As a photographer, you always hope for the best but expect the worst. To improve crane habitat, conservation groups have actually removed many trees that had grown on the islands. This has opened up the river for cranes.

Locals call the Anhinga the "snake bird" since only the head is seen when they are swimming on a pond. This bird was regularly fed little fish by a retired fellow in Florida. He always called "Gertie, Gertie, Gertie" when approaching it, so I did the same thing and got surprisingly close. These birds have been seen nesting as far north as southeastern Arkansas.

There are many, many water birds, each with unique ways of catching a meal of fish or other aquatic life. This group of birds is so diverse that it is hard to use a single definition to describe them. Some, like the Anhinga have feathers that resemble the scales of a lizard. Others, like the Least Tern, seem so sleek as to appear featherless. Some hunt alone while others form large groups and herd their quarry so all can feast.

Many families visit an ocean beach to watch and feed the gulls, never thinking about the complexity of flight and all the other birds that share this complex ecosystem. If you ever get a chance to see a breeding colony of terns and gulls, don't pass it up. The sounds and dynamics of the birds coming and going, the ritualistic displays and protective nature of the nesters will entertain you for hours. Non-bird watchers don't even see all the activity, or could care less. What a pity.

I try to time a trip to Florida each year in June, just to witness the colonies of nesting terns and gulls. Some inland states also have colony nesters. On the Missouri River bordering South Dakota and Nebraska, the U.S. Corps of Engineers monitors the colonies of Piping Plovers and Least Terns, both considered either "threatened" or "endangered" species. I was fortunate to make a trip with corps biologists to view conservation efforts that protect these birds from human encroachment. Public awareness and cooperation are vital to the program's success.

It is a known fact that humans like to relax and recreate around water. So, too, do many bird species. Sometimes the two come into serious conflict especially during nesting season. Only recently have groups come forward to help the birds. What would life be like without the birds that give birdwatchers so much pleasure. Would you want to live in a birdless world?

The Double-crested Cormorant is known to winter from Arkansas south to the Gulf. They nest from Nebraska northward. Some winter on Lake Bella Vista. Note the green eye.

Often considered a messy pest by dock owners, the Brown Pelican provides many memorable moments for the serious birdwatcher. Pelicans were using our waterways long before man began to compete for prime ocean- side real estate. Its like the debate of which came first the chicken or the egg. In this case, the pelican came first. Let us seriously take pleasure in watching this unique species as they go about feeding, resting, nesting and rearing their young.

The American White Pelican seems to prefer fresh water and can be seen in nesting colonies on lakes in north central parts of the country. They also nest in greater numbers in southern Canada. This photo was taken in June on the Missouri river near Yankton, South Dakota. They must be nonbreeders since they are not displaying a semi- circular growth on the top of their beaks. Typically, these birds do not dive like the Brown Pelican, preferring to swim in groups scooping up the fish.

American Oystercatchers are unusual in that they only occasionally feed on small fish, preferring mollusks and a variety of invertebrates. At high tides and in darkness they concentrate in large groups for security. Their nuptial displays include walking and posturing close together on a shoreline or in low-level flights, often attracting other pairs to join in. They nest on sand dunes, are monogamous and use the same site many years. Black Oystercathers are found on the West Coast.

The Black Skimmer has a most unusual method of capturing prey. The lower jaw, or mandible, is longer than the upper part of the bill. Flying with only the bill submerged, when a fish strikes the lower bill, the head doubles back, the bills close and the prey is swallowed. For this to work effectively the fish population needs to be quite high. In the evening or at night, small fish come to the surface making it easier for the skimmers. They nest in colonies with the terns and gulls.

A flock of flying "peeps." That's the term used when you are not sure. Probably Western Sandpipers and Least Sandpipers.

Shorebirds in winter plumage are difficult to identify. This photo was taken at St. Marks National Wildlife Refuge in Florida.

There's quite a size difference between the Willet and the Ruddy Turnstones digging for lunch. My favorite photo spot in Jacksonville is Huguenot Memorial Park Beach. I can put my camera on a window mount and photograph from the car.

On this day the beach was loaded with jellyfish. A Sanderling spent a lot of time investigating the dead speciman. Huguenot Park is also a breeding area for terns and gulls. It's a great place to photograph a variety of flying birds.

In February, when this picture was taken, the Ruddy Turnstones had not yet come into full breeding plumage. They winter on both coasts and nest far north on the arctic tundra and Alaska. During spring and fall migration, they have been recorded in almost every state. I have always admired them and have several wooden turnstone decoys to finish painting.

Only a very small percentage of bird species like the Spotted Sandpiper practice polyandry, where a female mates with several males, lays the eggs and leaves the males to incubate them. Phalarope females are also more colorful than the males who incubate and rear the broods. I was surprised to see this bird while waiting for the Canada Geese to hatch.

Royal Terns nest in the sand dunes north of Jacksonville, Florida. It's a great place to practice flight shots. They are so fast, it is difficult to get focused on them. Expect a small percentage of your exposures to be crisp. I have two lenses. The 200/400 Nikkor focuses fast. And if I can just stay on the bird, it will focus continuously. My 80/400 Nikon is very slow.

Another Royal Tern coming almost directly at me. This is the best picture out of twenty I took at this location. These birds are deceptively fast. As I remember, I used a monopod to help steady the camera lens. It weighs over seven pounds. While a monopod helps, they are not really easy to use when photographing flying birds. Often, I hand- hold, pan, shoot and rest.

It's hard to believe that these Least Terns weigh only 1.5 ounces. This pair is nesting on the Atlantic coast, but there is another group that nests on inland waterways in the central part of the country. The larger bird is probably the female. Males bring fish offerings, which is an important part of the courtship ritual. When nesting, these little birds can be very aggressive in keeping predators away. Making numerous accelerated passes, the flying terns are difficult to photograph.

These two photos of related species were taken on the same day on a muddy bay just off the Atlantic Ocean. If this bird was in breeding plumage it would be easier to identify. If the bill was yellow with a black tip and there were dark markings around the neck and forehead, you'd agree that this is a Piping Plover. The birds need our help to avoid extirpation.

Since their plumage changes little during the year, the Semipalmated Plover is much easier to identify. They nest farther north than the Piping Plover and migrate through most states. They winter on both the East and West Coast. Since they nest far away from human encroachment, their future is not threatened like the Least Tern and Piping Plover.

A pair of gulls really "laughing" it up! The name Laughing Gull fits them perfectly, as this photo shows. It was selected as Photo of the Week by Birder's World. Laughing Gulls join many other bird species that nest in the dunes at Huguenot Park. These gulls are highly gregarious and can usually be seen in large groups. They often "pick up" after humans.

Our most common white- headed gull, this bird shows the red markings that help identify it as a Ring- billed Gull. In addition to ocean beaches, they can be seen anywhere people dispose of garbage and trash, including parking lots. At our nearby lake, groups of them follow cormorants waiting to steal a fish or two from the agile underwater hunters.

Kingfishers are in a group by themselves. You'll find them around brackish water or fresh water, hunting alone from some vantage point where they can see their prey. Sometimes they hover until the time is right to make a dive. Their rate of success is above average. This female Belted Kingfisher has a cavity nest in a nearby creek bank. I have yet to find it.

While the Killdeer is lumped in with the shorebirds, you will find it near shorelines or in uplands far from water. This female had three two-day-old babies running around in this large rock garden. It would have been difficult to have found the nest as it was just a depression in the rocks. The eggs are perfectly colored to effectively foil discovery by predators.

When you see a band on a bird like this Bald Eagle, you can't help but wonder where the bird came from and where it has been. Once, I was close enough to photograph the numbers on a banded Snow Goose. What a story. The bird was 22.

EAGLES, HAWKS, OWLS AND VULTURES

Much published research has been done on the Birds of Prey. They are an intriguing and diverse group. Even Aristole wrote about them. The ancient sport of falconry has done much to inspire a great deal of curious interest. My first observation of raptors was as a teenager, watching "chicken hawks" soar over the Elkhorn river valley near Omaha, where we hunted ducks in the fall.

In 1974 I met two "falconers" in Lincoln, shot some film and photos for the Game Commission and became interested in the sport. One day, I discovered a little American Kestrel nearly drowned under my neighbor's sprinkler. I rescued her, got a license to keep her and became Nebraska's third falconer. Smallest of the true Falcons, she hardly fit the image of a hunting hawk. Little "Hawkeye" eagerly killed sparrows when I took her out hunting.

After a year, she became more independent, occasionally venturing out on her own. After a few days of unsuccessful hunting I would look out in the back yard to find her sitting on her perch waiting for a handout. It was a great experience for me and I was very happy when in the spring she found a mate and left for good.

Silent Spring, a book written by Rachel Carson in 1962 brought public awareness to the plight of eagles, hawks and other wildlife. The problems were directly related to the use of DDT and other hard pesticides. Because of reproductive problems and thin egg shells, Eagles and Peregrine Falcons were placed on the endangered list. DDT was banned and recovery efforts were put in place. I visited the Peregrine Falcon Recovery Center in Colorado Springs, run primarily by falconers from the Air Force Academy. That experience increased my interest in hawks even more. I supported that program and many others.

Thousands of bird watchers have visited Hawk Mountain in east- central Pennsylvania when the hawks are migrating through from September to December. In 2006, over 26,000 hawks, eagles, falcons and harriers were counted, the largest number in many years, attesting to the fact that conservation efforts are indeed working.

This juvenile Red- tailed Hawk is just off the nest. You can still see some downy feathers. It gets a red tail next year.

I couldn't resist taking this picture on a foggy morning. This is my resident female Red-Shouldered Hawk. You can see the deep separation over her brood patch. At 15 feet, I can actually see bare skin when she fluffs and preens her feathers.

I'm too old to climb a 32- foot extension ladder. I did it anyway but found I still was not able to look down into the nest. This is the second nest they've built in my yard. Last year, they nested across the street. They don't re- use old nests.

It is easy to tell the male Red- shouldered Hawk has something in his sights. I stock bullfrogs in my ponds to keep them here.

When he caught a frog, he flew up to the deck rail, then carried it off to a tree where the female had been waiting.

The female is much darker over all and after a quick dip in the pond she begins to preen the soft feathers around her brood patch.

After spending so many years in my yard, the hawks now let me open my office window to take pictures.

A wedding gift for a falconer friend who kept Prairie Falcons, this 1975 painting was modeled after one of his birds.

My only effort to paint a Screeh Owl. The eastern race is predominantly reddish while the western race is gray.

82

The diminutive Burrowing Owl follows prairie dogs around just so it can use an old underground burrow for a nesting place. They can be pretty aggressive, dive- bombing the dogs until they get the message that the owl means business.

Knowing that I needed flight shots of Turkey Vultures, I kept putting it off since I was seeing them every day. Finally, I spent three days chasing them around, waiting for a decent pose. They use the lift of thermals to soar almost effortlessly.

This bird, still on the roost, was using its dark wings to collect heat on a cold morning. They roost on everything from microwave towers, homes and boat covers to trees. Some people use scare tactics to drive them away, even "shell- crackers."

BIRDS OF FOREST AND YARD

Pileated Woodpeckers are early risers and very camera shy.

If you live in the woods or near the woods, you are lucky to have a front row seat to the "greatest show on earth." All you need is a few feeders and a bird book to help you identify the unnamed vagabonds—for that is the fun of it all—knowing all the birds that come to your yard and watching their antics. Birds are like circus performers—each has a special skill or talent.

The last time I saw a Red- breasted Nuthatch was eight years ago. It brought me special pleasure to see a pair of them visit my feeders again and I do my best to keep them coming. Knowing which food each species prefers is helpful. Some birds like to eat from a particular feeder while others prefer the ground. As with any other hobby, experience is the best way to learn each bird's preferences. You also learn to deal with the bullies—extra feeders help give everyone a chance.

It is also important to provide water for your visitors—a water heater is a must during extremely cold weather. Fortunately, I have three small ponds that make it easy for the birds to bathe and get a drink.

Almost all the photos in this section were taken in my yard. There's a picture of my set- up on page 130. I must confess that there are many birds that I haven't seen in my yard—only once did I see a Baltimore Oriole, or an Eastern Towhee. Warblers undoubtedly migrate through my woods, but I very seldom see one. Luckily, a Wilson's Warbler flitted around in a tree just outside my rear patio door long enough for me to grab a camera and click off two shots. See page 117.

Fall, winter and spring are the best times to lure birds to your yard. Sometimes, in the heat of summer, it almost seems like there are no birds around except for cardinals, chickadees and titmice. So you keep feeding even if the show is missing many key performers.

Surprisingly, for me, the Blue Jay became the most difficult subject to photograph. After years of trying, finally success.

For several years, I have had a few American Robins winter in my yard. They eat from the suet feeders and what ever they find on the ground. A masonite panel with a hole for my lens replaces the window glass in my bedroom. This is the reward.

The Blue Jay, robin and this cardinal were all photos taken from my bedroom. My wife tolerated the cold coming in around the plastic covering the lens hole. While some people photograph through glass windows, I could never do that.

"Orange on orange cardinal" was just one of those photo surprises.

I never realized how large a bluebird's eyes are.

They nest in my yard. See the baby on page 113.

The Carolina Wren takes top honors for its amazingly amusing antics.

The Tufted Titmouse is a year- around resident in my yard.

Indigo Buntings are not as secretive as the painted variety.

Painted Bunting populations have declined almost 3 percent a year since 1966. This banded male is part of a 5-year study.

Earliest of migrant arrivals in the spring, the Eastern Phoebe is a frequent nester under one of our rental properties. They usually bring off two broods of four young each. Being small and drab looking, a twitching tail is a key to its identity.

For a long time, I thought this was the Black- capped Chickadee that we had in Nebraska. The bird we have in Arkansas is the Carolina Chickadee. The giveaway is the smaller head, grayer wings and shorter tail. Their calls are different, too.

The Red-bellied Woodpecker is difficult for the beginning birdwatcher to identify since the red on the belly is very faint if it shows at all. The female, left, has some red on the back of the head, but not as much as the male.

The red patch on the back of the head shows this to be a male Downy Woodpecker. The Hairy is slightly larger.

Downies are a little timid and seem to hide behind a branch when approached with a camera. They visit the feeders daily.

For several years I anxiously waited to get occasional visits from a Northern Flicker. Finally, after placing this old stump on my patio and filling it with a cornmeal mix, a pair of Yellow-shafted Flickers became regular visitors, to my great pleasure.

What I didn't realize was the amount of damage a Yellow-bellied Sapsucker could do until a beautiful dogwood tree died in my back yard. When I inspected the trunk, I discovered hundreds of small holes drilled by a sapsucker. Female on left.

I never in my life expected a pair of White- breasted Nuthatches to nest in my yard.   Great fun watching them come and go to the little bird house just fifteen feet from my office window. I was treated to all of the intricate displays like "bill wiping."

It is a real treat to have Red- breasted Nuthatches spend the winter in Arkansas. Some say it means their food source up north is scarce. It had been almost eight years since I saw one in my yard. I hope I won't have to wait that long again.

While I have never seen a Scarlet Tanager in my yard, Summer Tanagers come every year. I have yet to discover a nest.

This female Summer Tanager is very elusive and difficult to photograph. I often see the bright male, but rarely do I see her.

Pine Siskins travel in loose flocks and are infrequent visitors to my feeders. This is a female. The male has yellow wing bars, rather than white as this female displays. They nest far north to Alaska, but winter from Minnesota south to Florida.

Typically, you hear the Gray Catbird before you see it in the thick underbrush. I coaxed this one out in the open because it seemed to like the recipe I use for my "mish mash." They don't sit for long so you have to be pretty quick on the trigger.

What most people call a "snow bird" is actually a Dark-eyed Junco. Juncos appear in many different color variations. This female is the "slate colored" with no distinction between the color of the body and the color of the head. Males are darker.

There are two color variations of the White- throated Sparrow. Some have a tan stipe and some have bright yellow eye brows and white stripes. This is the duller adult. I used to get a bigger variety of sparrows at my feeders in Nebraska.

House Sparrows do not venture into the woods of Northwest Arkansas and we see only an occasional starling. We do have House Finches, another transplant which competes with the Purple Finch. It is difficult to tell the difference beween them.

When the Myrtle Yellow- rumped Warbler comes in the fall it is drab in color. As spring approaches, they get their bright breeding plumage. This adult is just beginning to get it's color. Males will be much bluer and show yellow on their heads.

The winter plumage of both male and female Goldfinch is very much the same. Color of a breeding male is unmistakable.

Twitching wings and tail of the Hermit Thrush can help identify this ground dweller. The camera captured it perfectly.

Eastern Bluebirds visit the suet feeders every day during the winter. Sometimes as many as six or eight jocky for position in the feeding order. They nest in large numbers on our eight local golf courses. The Bluebird Society monitors their success.

It wasn't long since this little one left the nesting box. While taking on the coloration of a bluebird, at this stage it is difficult to tell if this is a male or female. Because of concerned groups, the Eastern Bluebird has shown a population increase.

I had to call a Painted Bunting expert to see if this was a young male or mature female. Sometimes during the year, it is difficult to tell them apart. Consensus was that this is indeed a female. One could hardly mistake a breeding male.

A rare visitor to the feeding area was this female Indigo Bunting.   They, like their painted cousins, prefer millet to any other seed.   They both nest close to the ground.   I have never discovered a nest.   There must have been one in or near my yard.

It is truly an art to get outstanding photos of hummingbirds. We only get Ruby- throated Hummingbirds here in Arkansas.

A migrating male Wilson's Warbler paused just long enough for this picture. They are noted for their continuous motion.

On a snowy, cold morning at Halsey National Forest in Nebraska, a few male Sharp-tailed Grouse showed up on the traditional booming grounds. Strutting and displaying takes place from late March until May, when all the hens have been bred.

BIRDS OF PRAIRIE AND FARM

In the 1800's, homesteaders crossing the vast prairies of the United States were treated to great numbers of wild birds, which provided critical nourishment. Many areas boasted large populations of Wild Turkey, Sharp-tailed grouse, Prairie-Chickens, Quail and myriad valuable waterfowl species. It was a time of plenty and so everyone assumed we had an unlimited supply of birds to keep the larders full. There was a great demand for wild meat in eastern markets. Oldtimers tell of trains hauling thousands of barrels of salted-down grouse. Market hunters were only too willing to kill hundreds of birds a day with their large shotguns. Birds were shot year around with no thought of conservation.

By the early 1900's, states organized game management agencies to set seasons and bag limits for all game birds. Game wardens were given the responsibility to enforce all the regulations passed by state governments. Game numbers were so low, hunting was totally prohibited and it was many years before any season was opened, if at all.

The Ring-necked Pheasant had been transplanted from China and in the 1920's the first regular hunting seasons were opened. Conditions experienced during the dust bowl with failing farming ventures actually resulted in a pheasant population explosion. The only other gamebird to benefit from the plow and crop land was the Prairie-Chicken.

What happened in North Dakota pretty much summerizes what has taken place in the rest of the country. North Dakota had no Prairie-Chickens until the settlers plowed up the prairie to plant grain crops. Greater Prairie-Chickens moved in to take advantage of food that would carry them over the harsh winter months. As farming intensified and more prairie was lost, Prairie-Chicken numbers fell drastically. The last "Heath Hen, a relative of the Prairie-Chicken was seen in 1932 near Nantucket Island where it once lived.

Other related populations, including the Lesser Prairie-Chicken and the endangered Attwater's Prairie-Chicken, were reduced to dangerously low levels, due mostly to human encroachment and habitat destruction. Biologists have reintroduced birds in several states with limited success.

Sharp-tailed Grouse originally ranged from Alaska and Canada to as far south as Oklahoma, east to Wisconsin and Michigan and west to Montana. Their numbers, like the Prairie-Chicken are alarmingly low. In areas where they traditionally harvested up to 100,000 grouse per year, the number has dropped to 1,000 grouse. Over-grazing and other factors have caused this dramatic population decline.

Oklahoma is one of the States to have documented bird populations in a Breeding Bird Atlas. I refer to my copy often because what is happening in Oklahoma is probably a similar trend in nearby states. It was reported in 1923 that while having been numerous earlier, Sharp-tailed Grouse were now rare. The population trend for the Prairie-Chicken is the same—while Oklahoma has both the Lesser and Greater, the numbers are so low, no hunting is allowed.

On the other hand, species like the Wild Turkey have shown a significant population increase, due in large part to game managers who have reintroduced turkeys back into traditional habitat. Northern Bobwhite quail originally increased their range as trees and brush started growing along cropland and streams, creating favorable habitat for the expansion. Harsh winters lower quail numbers while mild winters and mild weather during nesting help increase numbers. Hunting has little effect if the entire covey is not harvested. Quail numbers, like those of most bird species in Oklahoma, have shown an average decrease of one percent per year during the survey period 1966 to 2000. It is a trend that concerns both game and non-game biologists.

Another photographer, Bill Bussen, invited me to his carpeted blind to view and photograph the Greater Prairie-Chickens on a lek near Norton, Kansas. At least 20 males were on hand to impress the four hens that came to select the perfect mate.

If Benjamin Franklin had his way, the Wild Turkey would have been our national symbol. Because of good management practices, turkey populations are increasing in states where they have been reintroduced. They were almost gone in 1900.

Very few people, even some game biologists, have ever seen a cock Ring- necked Pheasant display while it's trying to impress a prospective mate. My father raised ringnecks at our home in Omaha so I saw the display often.   I loved to watch the males compete for small harems on the outskirts of Lincoln.   Since hens are not hunted they should far outnumber cocks.

I photographed this White- winged Dove in Sioux City, Iowa, of all places. Taxes generated by the sale of shotguns, ammunition and other related hunting equipment are used to buy, protect and manage habitat that benefits many, many non- game birds and wildlife. The elusive Mourning Dove is also hunted, requiring the purchase of much ammunition.

The prairies and farm land offer the birdwatcher a chance to see species that can't be seen in town. It is easy for a novice to confuse a Dickcissel (above) with a Meadowlark. The Red-winged Blackbird (top) nests wherever there is a marsh or large wet area. Few realize that the Loggerhead Shrike (bottom) can prey on lizards, snakes and small birds. They often hang a kill on a sharp thorn and feed on it later.

Watching the acrobatic maneuvers of a Scissor-tailed Flycatcher chasing a flying insect is a sight to behold. Don't miss it.

125

A bird of the roadside, the Eastern Kingbird must find a good living feeding on the insects escaping mowers and cars.

Normally displaying a raucous nature, this Northern Mockingbird seems relaxed, showing only a hint of mischief in the eye.

The range of the Greater Roadrunner is larger than most people think. Thought to be a bird of arid land only, I have seen several of them two miles from the border of Akansas and Missouri. A friend in Fayetteville, Arkansas, had a pair for years.

Barn Swallows are widely distributed and once built their nests in caves. They have adapted well to man, so nesting in natural sites is rarely seen. Barn Swallow populations are remaining fairly stable. A deeply forked tail identifies them.

My backyard photo set looks pretty junky but the birds don't seem to mind. Even the ground feeders get used to the platform I provide. Changing props and backgrounds is easy and necessary so all the photos don't look the same.

PHOTOGRAPHY INSIGHTS AND COMMENTS

Wildlife photography is more about patience and effort than photo equipment. Buy the best camera and lens you can afford, then concentrate on your technique and skills. I started out with and have always used a totally manual camera and when I talk to experienced photographers, I find that a large percentage of them use the manual mode. It forces you to know how the camera works. Using fully automatic settings will give you consistantly good images, but often, the results are not what you are looking for.

My back yard is really a stage set with painted background panels, props and perches. The table top puts the birds at ground level for the camera—I don't have to lay on my belly. A flash helps soften the shadows. You can see my "mish mash" pasted to the back side of the logs and limbs.

My granddaughter and birding buddy, Grace. When she was seven she said, "Gramps, you need some good binoculars. I can make you a pair out of two toilet paper tubes. They are really good and easy to make." I still have mine.

Many of the bird photos in this book were taken on this set, or another one on the south side of our house. The master bedroom, which faces south, also provided a higher angle after I put a plywood piece with a lens hole in the window opening. It did let cold air in, so my wife could hardly wait 'til it came down. My office window, facing west, also provided a great place to photograph the Red- shouldered Hawks. They became very tolerant of me even though I was just fifteen feet away from their favorite perch.

When the hawks first started showing up, I was still using my manual Nikon FM with a 100/600 milimeter zoom lens. My first transparencies of mating hawks were ruined by the processor. That is when I decided to switch to digital equipment. Now, I have total control of the process and don't have to worry about scratches or lint on my slides. I am enjoying photography now more than ever.

The best tip I can give a novice is to always have your camera in the car. Can't say that I have followed that advice all the time, since I have missed some great shots because I didn't have a camera handy. Also, spend some money on a window mount. Many published photos have been taken from cars. Cars make great photo blinds. Some of my best shots were taken from an open car window.

With all of the new digital technology and sophisticated equipment, everyone can be an instant expert photographer. In fact, there are so many excellent photos taken, the publishing market is flooded with them. Many people get into photography thinking that they will make a good living. Only a very few are successful selling their work.

There is no doubt that photographing birds makes you a birdwatcher rather than a birder. Being a birdwatcher helps you learn the true behavior and the more unusual characteristics of birds. It teaches you to see birds.

SCULPTURES IN WOOD & CLAY

In 1982, after seeing my first brick sculpture at Endicott Clay products, I decided to try my hand at creating three large panels for Rock Creek Station State Historical Park near Fairbury, Nebraska. At the time, I was carving wooden birds for private collectors across the nation. In fact, I was very encouraged by winning several blue ribbons in the professional class at the annual World Wildfowl Carving Competition in Ocean City, Maryland.

To my surprise, it wasn't long until most of my commissions were for brick scuptures. The *Fighting Eagles*, which set a new benchmark, was featured on the cover of the Brick Institute's special publication sent to every architect in the nation.

During the 24 years I sculpted in clay, I completed hundreds of architectural commissions, including many for large corporations and several Federal, state and local agencies. I was fortunate to visit several countries where my sculptures were being installed.

Sculpting in leather- hard, unfired brick was difficult work...on some projects, a ton or more of clay had to be cut away by hand before the commission was completed. Working on a sculpture for Disney World, I fell off of a scaffold and had to take a break to visit the emergency ward for multiple stitches in my head.

At sixty- five, I was fortunate to work on my first bronze sculpture project for the Omaha Zoo's Safari Park near Omaha, Nebraska. The deadline was rather tight, so it was necessary to contract with three different foundries to meet the production schedule. Since one was in West Palm Beach, Florida, one in Sante Fe, New Mexico, and one in Pueblo, Colorado, I managed to log 40,000 miles on my car along with countless air miles. I completed nine larger than life buffalo: five bulls, two cows and two young cavorting calves.

After moving to Arkansas, my interest in photography was rekindled. I purchased digital equipment and began concentrating on this book.

132

The extreme relief and detail set a new benchmark for brick sculptors.

This buffalo is eight feet tall and was sculpted in white foam and coated with clay. A rubber mold was made and filled with three- eights of an inch of wax. The wax pieces were encased in a silica shell. Wax was melted out of the shell and molten bronze filled the void.

We call this a Blue Goose, but it is a morph or color phase of the Snow Goose. In order to capture every detail accurately, I had a taxidemist mount a bird in this position. Some people call bird carvers model makers, but in reality, we are just trying to duplicate nature in a life- like way. It took three weeks to complete and won a blue ribbon at the World competition. This bird was three pieces of wood, glued and hollowed out to make it lighter and float realistically.

"Flying Doves" was more of a sculpture or mobile than a carving. The grasses were fabricated from brass rods and copper that moved when the air was disturbed. People said that in this life- sized composition, I captured the essence of the doves.

Cedar Waxwings have always fascinated me. This too, was as much of a sculpture as it was a carving. The berries were fashioned from plumbers epoxy while the vines were brass welding rods with copper leaves.

Over the years, I carved six loons. They are a surprisingly large bird, measuring 32 inches overall with a body length of about 24 inches and 12 inches wide. That is a lot of wood. While many wildfowl carvers switched to tupelo harvested from the swamps of Louisiana, I always prefered to carve in jelutong, a dense wood from the forests of Malaysia. This, like many other woods is becoming hard to locate. The owner of this bird lives in loon country and does annual loon surveys for the state.

Another challenging carving was the Ross's Goose. There was much detail in the primary feathers extending beyond the tail. Painting an all white bird is more difficult, too. The "World" Coot winners were always "cajuns" of Louisiana. More than a few eyebrows were raised when a Nebraskan won the blue ribbon. The Blue-winged Teal on top was my very first realistic carving. The bird on the bottom was carved two years later in 1981. My carving skills had improved considerably.

How could I ever forget this carving of a Black- billed Magpie and Prairie Racerunner. From the moment I picked up a fresh road- killed bird in Colorado, bagged it, iced it down and drove 500 miles home, all I could think about was doing this carving. It was showcased in the foyer of an upscale house in Omaha. To top it off, the woman beat me down in price. While the Atlantic Puffin looks like a simple carving, the bird and all the fish were carved out of one piece of wood.

The Redhead taking off was a challenging piece. There are 10 primary and 10 secondary feathers on each wing, not to mention all of the other feathers that help keep the bird flying. Knowing the anatomy and subtle nuances that bring life to the bird has always been my goal. Here again, I sold this bird too cheaply but my satisfaction always comes from people liking my work well enough to want to purchase it. This bird has a home in a prestigious office in Omaha.

This Whooping Crane was featured on the cover of the Omaha World Herald's "Magazine of the Midlands." My intention was to carve several of them but completing this one proved to be tedious and time consuming. They are, after all, the tallest North American bird. Carving raptors like the little Sparrow Hawk took less time but were just as enjoyable. I taught carving lessons to beginners, but it was frustrating trying to help people find the bird in a block of wood.

This carving started out to be a half-sized Bald Eagle. Then the Red-shouldered Hawks started perching on a branch just fifteen feet from my window. It quickly became a carving of my favorite hawk.

I carved many Pheasants because the bird is so popular with hunters. They are very difficult to paint accurately. This male Shoveler duck was my best attempt at capturing its true beauty. Looking back, my first Shoveler was pretty primitive.

Bobwhites disturbed while dusting was probably my most complex carving. It was purchased by a serious collector in Indiana.

EPILOGUE

They say that 60 percent of the people start at the back of a book or magazine. If you are one of those, you are reading the most important thing about me and my career as an artist. Before I was born, God knew me, even every hair on my head—He knew what I was and what I would become. He also knew that I would always be His.

As I look back over my life, I can see how God had control of me and my destiny. So many things that happened, didn't happen by chance. He was directing me, guiding me and most of all, loving me with an unrelenting love. My sins must have hurt him deeply, and yet he always forgave me. I know Christ died for my sins.

Many times over the years I did thank God for the talent He gave me—once, in particular, I remember bowing my head and praising him for his many blessings and for the fact that He helped me sculpt a flying eagle out of a big block of clay bricks, and do it so quickly.

When I was in the third grade, He helped me win a city-wide Easter poster contest. All through the years, my art ability opened doors and gave me opportunities to show my talents. In the military, on every assignment, my art always got me daytime duties. At Offutt Air Force Base, the Provost Sergeant saw my talent and moved me into the office just so I could help plan and draw up the new traffic design for SAC headquarters.

It was no accident that my transfer orders were changed from the Air Base in Little Rock, Arkansas, to Omaha. If not, I would never have met Marilyn, my wife, in the art classes at the University of Nebraska at Omaha. We were married in 1961. God brought us together for a reason. We both know why and we give Him thanks each day.

The twenty years at the Game and Parks Commission went by quickly. What I remember most is that during the early 80's, we were establishing canoe trails on the rivers of Nebraska. The director, Gene Mahoney, would lead groups of dignitaries on weekend trips on the Snake, Dismal, Blue and many other waterways. On Sunday mornings, I led impromptu church services on some sandbar or shoreline. Not surprisingly, I picked up the nickname of *Reverend*. I didn't feel all that religious at the time but simply had the need to share my God-given faith with others.

One morning I was sitting in my carving studio, wondering how I would get more carving commissions after those I had were completed. Truly, the Lord inspired me to make sketches of those carvings I'd like to do in the future. I printed and mailed 500 copies of three different sketch books and the orders came in. Thanks be to God.

INDEX OF BIRD ILLUSTRATIONS